The Self Wanders

Elena Tzilini

BookLeaf Publishing

India | USA | UK

Presentation by *BookLeaf Publishing*

Web: www.bookleafpub.com

E-mail: info@bookleafpub.com

ISBN: 9789360947842

First edition 2024

Table of Contents

I. CONFLICT

Unwritten Pages

I wake up, get up and sit
No time to waste, no time to breathe

The book of my life is closed and blank
The words unwritten a thousand and one

Don't know from where to begin
Don't recall when I run out of ink

There is so much more to say
But time doesn't want to stay

Wake up, wake up
Write another page

Sit down, sit down
It won't work any other way

What's the point anyway?

Uncertainly Certain

Perhaps it's meant to be
It must be
Maybe that's the path
I know it is
There are chances I was wrong
I'm sure I was not
You seem very sure
How sure are you?
I can tell you what I believe
I can't tell you what I feel
What is certain and what is not?
At the end we think we know it all

Boiling Pot

I'm boiling like a pot
Forgotten on the stove
What I carry inside
You'll never know
Everything is burned
By the hand I once held

The Dialogue

Stand up right, talk it out
I don't want to, shut it now
Volume up, get it out
I only know how

You're so shy, speak to me
Can't you see I'm busy?
With what though? What's your world?
You're not the one to know

Keep it tight to your needs
I keep it to my dreams
Think again, you will fail
At least I won't be dead

You're so strange, you need a change
I'm myself, what's to blame?
How's that good? That ain't cool
I'm sorry your mind is full

Where are you going? You can't leave
I'm the captain of my ship
Be careful then, blue can turn red
Every colour is in my palette

I'm Sorry, But

I'm sorry, but I can no longer lie
I'm sorry, but that's not alright
I'm sorry, but I have a life
I'm sorry, but the fault ain't mine
I'm sorry, but after everything I've done
I'm sorry, but you never saw my heart
I'm sorry, but I'm leaving this time
I'm sorry, but I've lost my mind
I'm sorry, but all that's yours is mine
I'm sorry, but I was expecting this for a while
I'm sorry, but there is a taxi outside
I'm sorry, but I'm gone

You're sorry, but I'm not anymore

II. CONFUSION

Up I Fly, Down I see

Up I fly, down I see
Down in the endless dark blue sea.
Endless, but not for long
As light comes in, dressed like a small dot.

A lonely man perhaps lives there
A man I do not know or ever will.
Perhaps his children came for a visit
Perhaps he's lonely and cold.

Another dot appears
Another life disappears.
Dark blue, yellow and green
These are the colours we live in.

And before I know it
Up here where I think.
The yellow dots are more than I can count
Lost men and women are now found.

Connected in the eyes of the sky
Still isolated in their own little lives.
And although I think I'm flying
Deep down I know, one of them is mine.

It won't be long
Till I'm back home.
And the faces I've forgotten,
are not deserted anymore.

We'll join our brightest corners of our souls
We'll invite darkness to our homes.
Don't ask how from the window seat I know
That there is no dot and nowhere to go.

Down I fly, up I see
Everything turning into darkness.
Every man back to his loneliness
There is nothing here to see.

I'm Afraid

I'm afraid
I'm afraid of what is yet to come
I'm afraid of what's left and what's right
I'm afraid of the passage of time
I'm afraid of what I saw when I was blind
I'm afraid of your fading into the dark
I'm afraid of death and the end of life
I'm afraid of those who are still alive
I'm afraid of being alone and trapped
I'm afraid of having nowhere to hide
I'm afraid of who I'll become by night
I'm afraid

A Hundred Ways

When I was lost
You showed me the way.
None of them belonged to me
But all screamed my name.

And yet, the path I took
There is nowhere to be found
It got lost with me too
And I miss its hunting sound.

I wake up today
In another path, another land.
Is life still the same?
Or is it me who really changed?

I'm still not sure if I did right.
Can I go back? Can I see forward?
Why did I go left, instead of right?
I'm tired of living in fast-forward.

I'm lost again
Please show me another way
Whatever it is, I'll follow
Wherever it is, it's my way

Grey

What have I done to only see grey?
To have erased all the colours of the universe
and be left to imagine

The deep red of the blooming rose,
In the hands of an old man still in love
The infinite blue of the dark sea,
Where small paper boats are floating free
The calming green of earth and its leaves,
Absorbing the warmth and life
Of the bright yellow of the morning sun,
Burning the dusty white pages of the story
That was once mine

I still remember the black of the ink,
That went dry that cold, starry night
Leaving its last drop on the grey areas
Of a lost life

A Second Chance

Give me a moment to breathe

Give me a second chance to live

The leaves are still green and growing big

The flowers blossom in bright pink

The sea infinite and free

Like the birds flying above me

And my ignorance

III. COMFORT

Last Day Of The Moon

It's late, quarter past ten
Another day, it's gone before it sets
There is a feeling in the air I cannot explain
The moon is up, but it's feeling down
I feel for it and I want to drawn

The breeze is piercing through my skin
My eyes are closing, but I want to stay awake
The moon is full, but incomplete
This day will never come again
And if it's the moon's last day, I will stay

Or perhaps it's time to go to bed
To find a star to give the blame
Be with someone that doesn't look down
Like the moon does on me
And the blamed star on my crown

Nature's Call

Rain drops, wind blows
Right between your tiptoes
Touches your face, sings to your ear
You can't deny it, it must be real

And rain gets stronger and stronger
Your two pure eyes, full of water
You feel like you can't see clear
While it washes away your fear

And everything you dreamed of
Everything you wished
It's now right in front of you
Screaming for you to leave

Don't let the sun burn
What your soul just felt
it doesn't rain everyday
So don't rely on what they say

And wind runs through your skin
Your heart skips another beat
You feel like you're dying when
Your old soul is trying to live again

It will feel weird
It will feel surreal
Your truth is right here
You just need to hear

She Sees The Sea

I see the sea
As she sees me
The sea sees here
Through her shield
She swims in the sea
She's the only one I see
Myself is finally seen
As she sings to me
And the silent sea
I can no longer see
The sea then asks the sun
To shine on our ship
The sunset sees us both
As we swim in infinite sleep

The Blanket

Ahh

I love this smell
Of the hot black coffee
First thing in the morning

I love this touch
Of the warm blanket
The cold night's last act

Whatever the time
I need something
For my frozen heart

IV. CONFUSION

The Steps In Between

The city is empty, no sign of life
  The sky is dark while I'm holding your
  hand

I make a step forward
  You make a step back

I see a street light next to a wracked old car
I want to touch it, to warm up my heart
  You see nothing, you want to get in
  and run

I make two steps forward
  You make four steps back

I'm trying to not let go and keep holding your hand
  When I realise you were never holding
  me back

Oh Mother

Oh mother!
Where are you?
I saw you again
But you weren't there

With your eyes on the phone
And mine lost in thought
They couldn't meet each other
Like the day I was born

Oh mother!
Why is it so hard?
For us to live in the moment
And hold it tight?

When I'm with you and when I'm not
I miss you the same
But the moment I miss you the most
Is when I write what I didn't say

Oh mother!
I hope one day we meet for real
And forgive each other
And it's me again, your kid.

Like A Fly

Here I am again
Foggy sky
Window seat
Cannot sleep

Where did I go?
Who put me here?
I miss home
Just get me there

Can I stop?
Moving around
Like a fly
Above the ground

Here I come
Do I belong?
I feel better
Till I'm gone

Again
And again
And again
I'll be flying

Like a fly
Lost in the sky

Lost Bird

The feathers of my life
Are travelling with the wind
Wherever it blows, they follow
No purpose, no dreams

They touch faces and hands
Trying to find some land
To grow freedom and feed the soul
Of the bird that lost them all

It wasn't its fault, you know
When the blue-lighted faces in high street
Become one with the blue sky above
The bird doesn't know what it sees anymore

And I miss the times when
Our feathers were stronger than men
Our hearts softer than the seeds we plant
We are the lost bird

The End

This is the end
The boat has turned
Not back in time
But down in vain